A CENTURY
OF STORIES
NEW HANOVER COUNTY PUBLIC LIBRARY
1906-2006

Living in a World of
brown
Where Survival Means Blending In

Tanya Lee Stone

BLACKBIRCH PRESS, INC.

WOODBRIDGE, CONNECTICUT

For Jake, my animal lover, who wants there
to be A World of Yellow!

Published by Blackbirch Press, Inc.
260 Amity Road
Woodbridge, CT 06525

Email: staff@blackbirch.com
Web site: www.blackbirch.com

©2001 by Blackbirch Press, Inc.
First Edition

Printed in the United States

10 9 8 7 6 5 4 3 2 1

Photo Credits: All images ©Corel Corporation, except:
pages 6, 7: ©Digital Stock Corp.; pages 18, 20:
©PhotoDisc, Inc.

   Library of Congress Cataloging-in-Publication Data
Stone, Tanya Lee.
Living in a world of brown / by Tanya Lee Stone.
       p.   cm.
Summary: Introduces ten animals that rely on their brown
camouflage to survive in deserts, woods, or grasslands.
ISBN 1-56711-582-9 (hardcover: alk. paper)
1. Soil animals —Juvenile literature. 2. Grassland animals—
Juvenile literature. 3. Forest animals—Juvenile literature.
[1. Soil animals. 2. Grassland animals. 3. Forest animals.
4. Animals. 5. Camouflage (Biology)] I. Title.
QL110.S76 2001
591.47'2—dc21   2001002674

Contents

What do all of the animals in this book have in common? They all live in a world of brown. They make their homes in Earth's sand, dirt, and trees of deserts, woods, and grasslands. The 10 animals in this book are perfectly suited to their environments. Each relies on camouflage to survive. When something is camouflaged, it blends into its surroundings and is difficult to see. Camouflage helps these animals find food and escape danger. How do they do it?

Did You Know?

- Several kinds of whiptails lay eggs that are not fertilized by a male whiptail. These kinds of whiptails only produce female lizards.

- Whiptails can run up to 15 miles per hour (24 kilometers per hour).

4

Leopard and Whiptail Lizards

Desert Darters

Leopard and whiptail lizards are well camouflaged for their surroundings. Both reptiles live in desert areas where there are only scattered bushes. Whiptails are a light color with darker stripes and spots. They have long, whip-like tails.

These fast lizards zip around the desert and are hard to see. The leopard lizard has a yellowish—or grayish—brown color with spotted markings. This coloring blends into either sand or gravel. It is also hard to spot a leopard lizard crouched underneath a spindly shrub. Such camouflage helps the leopard do what it does best—launch surprise attacks on prey (animals it eats). Its camouflage also helps it when in danger. A leopard lizard will dart underneath a bush and stay still. A passing enemy will never know the lizard is there.

Did You Know?

- The roar of a lion is so loud it can be heard 5 miles away!

- Female lions do most of the hunting. Male lions protect the pride (a group of lions).

Lions

Camouflaged Creepers

Many grassland animals are always on the lookout for a lion attack. But, the "King of the Jungle" is not the world's greatest hunter. Lions cannot run fast for very long. Many of the animals they hunt, however, are swift runners. A lion actually catches its prey less than half of the time. When it does succeed, it's usually because it creeps up close to an animal through the tall grasses. Its light golden color camouflages the big cat and helps it hide from its prey. When the lion is ready to pounce, it takes its victim by surprise. Lion cubs are also camouflaged. The spots on their light brown fur help the babies hide from predators in the grass. When the cubs grow older, their spots fade away.

Did You Know?

A cottontail can run up to 18 miles per hour (29 kilometers per hour) when fleeing danger.

Cottontail Rabbits

Blending Bunnies

Have you ever seen a cotton-tail rabbit while you were taking a walk in the woods? Did it freeze in place as soon as it saw you coming? Cottontails stop in their tracks when they sense danger. If a rabbit stands still, a predator might not see it. The brown color of a cottontail's fur helps the

rabbit blend into the bushes or trees in the background. A cottontail can also escape a predator by dashing into some nearby brush. Running in a zig-zag pattern can confuse its enemy long enough for the cottontail to get away. Once safely in its hiding place, the color of its fur helps it to disappear.

Did You Know?

- Arizona is the rattlesnake capital of America.
- Every time a rattlesnake sheds its skin, it adds another rattle.

10

Rattlesnakes

Rock 'n Rattle

Rattlesnakes are named for the rattles at the ends of their tails. Watch out if you hear that rattle! The sound is a warning the snake sends when it is about to strike. The banded rock rattlesnake lives in rocky areas of Arizona and parts of Mexico. Its coloring is perfect for blending into its rock-covered background. During the day, these stone-colored snakes often hide from predators by slipping under rocks. The bands around its body make it look like it is many different pieces, rather than one long snake. This makes it even harder to see out in the open. When the snake needs to warm itself up on a cooler day, it can sun itself on top of a rock. Its coloring helps keep it safe by blending in to the rocky surroundings.

Did You Know?

Snout butterflies are related to butterflies that flew 70 million years ago in the days of dinosaurs.

Snout Butterflies

Invisible Insects

When you think of butterflies, you probably imagine dazzling patterns and bright colors. But the snout butterfly is different. It is usually a dull brownish color. When its wings are open, you might see two pretty orange spots on its wings. Most of the time, however, the snout butterfly sits on a tree branch or twig with its wings folded. It even lowers its antennae for better camouflage. Its shape and color look like a dead leaf to a predator—or even a person walking past. The snout butterfly is named for the long, furry, nose-like extensions it uses to sense whether it has found food.

Unlike the snout butterfly, most butterflies have bright patterns and colors on their wings.

13

Did You Know?

Nighthawks often lay their eggs on flat, gravel-covered rooftops when they can't find a natural habitat.

14

Nighthawks
Nifty Nesters

Most birds lay eggs in nests they build high off the ground. The common nighthawk, however, lays its eggs right on the ground.

It chooses a bare spot in the forest or a clearing in a field. This makes it an easier target for enemies. The nighthawk, though, has excellent camouflage for protection. The nighthawk's coloring blends into the ground perfectly. It has black, white, gray, and tan feathers. These colors help the bird to match different shades of rocks, grasses, plants, and sand. They also blend in well with wood and tree bark, making nighthawks hard to see while perched on fences and tree branches.

Did You Know?

Bull snakes are constrictors— they kill their prey by squeezing it to death.

Bull Snakes
Masterful Mimics

Bull snakes live in deserts, prairies, forests, and grasslands. Some of these habitats have wide-open spaces. Others offer plenty of places to hide. The bull snake's coloring camouflages it well in any of these environments. With its brown and black markings, a bull snake can easily hide in brush or in a tree. Its coloring helps this slow-moving snake avoid predators, such as eagles, hawks, foxes, and coyotes. Its good camouflage also helps it surprise its prey. Bull snakes also use a type of camouflage called mimicry—looking or acting just like another animal. When threatened, a bull snake makes a hissing sound and flattens its head. By doing this, the it is trying to convince an enemy that it is a rattlesnake so the enemy will leave it alone.

Many snakes use leaves and brush as hiding places.

Did You Know?

- A white-tailed deer can run up to 40 miles per hour (64 kilometers per hour).
- The white-tailed deer is named for the white color on the back of its tail. When there is danger, the deer raises its tail to signal others. This also helps a fawn follow its mother to safety.

White-tailed Deer

Dappled Deer

If you walk through the woods, you might find signs of a white-tailed deer. You might see a bed it made underneath a tree. Or notice buds nibbled off branches along a path. But chances are, the deer smelled you coming and went into hiding. The color of its coat helps to hide it well. In winter, its coat is a grayish brown that blends in with the duller colors of the season. When spring comes, the deer's coat changes to a reddish brown. This better matches the brightening background of the forest. Fawns (baby deer) are born with white spots. For the first few weeks, a fawn stays in its forest bed. Its spots help the fawn blend in with the dappled dots of sunlight and shadows that form in the woods. This blending helps to keep fawns safe from predators.

Did You Know?

Prairie dogs communicate with many different kinds of calls and barks. They have different sounds to signal danger, that the coast is clear, and even what kind of predator is lurking nearby.

Prairie Dogs

Burrow Builders

Prairie dogs are not dogs at all; they are cousins of the squirrel. But they do live on short-grass prairies. These animals stay away from areas with tall or thick grasses so they can have a better view of approaching enemies. Prairie dogs live in large family groups. They also build large underground towns, or burrows, with connecting tunnels. They build small mounds at entrances to a town and clip the grass down low with their teeth. These entrance mounds are not difficult to see. But it can be very hard to spot a sand-colored prairie dog poking its head out of a mound. Lookouts that poke their heads out of guard mounds also mark excellent places for other prairie dogs to make a quick getaway down a tunnel.

Did You Know?

- Bitterns lay creamy greenish eggs that stay well hidden in their marsh nest.
- Bitterns rarely leave their thick grass hideaways. They talk to each other with calls that can sound like thunder or the beating of a drum.

American Bitterns

Blending Birds

The American bittern is one of the hardest birds to see in the wild. This slow-flying bird relies on excellent camouflage to hide from enemies. Its feathers are brown, yellow, and black—all the different colors needed to blend into a wetland. A bittern also has stripes on its throat and chest. When it is threatened, it points its beak to the sky so its stripes disappear into the background of the tall grasses. This bird even sways its body back and forth to look like the windblown reeds. To hunt, it stands still, hidden in the grass, and waits for a frog, insect, or small fish to pass by. Then it snatches the prey in its bill.

Baby bitterns

GLOSSARY

Camouflage Any behavior or appearance that helps disguise an animal in its environment.

Mimicry When an animal copies the behavior, smell, or appearance of another animal.

Predator An animal that hunts other animals for food.

Prey An animal that is hunted by another animal.

Pride A group of lions.

FOR MORE INFORMATION

Books

Kalman, Bobbie. *How Do Animals Adapt?* New York, NY: Crabtree Publishing, 2000.

Kitchen, Bert. *Animal Lives: The Rabbit.* New York, NY: Larousse Kingfisher Chambers, Inc., 2000.

Schraer, William D., Herbert J. Stoltze. *Biology: Study of Life.* Upper Saddle River, NJ: Prentice Hall School Group, 1995.

Stonehouse, Bernard. *Camouflage.* New York, NY: Scholastic Trade, 2001.

Web Site

Learn more about animals at:

http://animal.discovery.com/search/results.jsp?channel=APL&srchtxt=animals

INDEX

mL

7/06